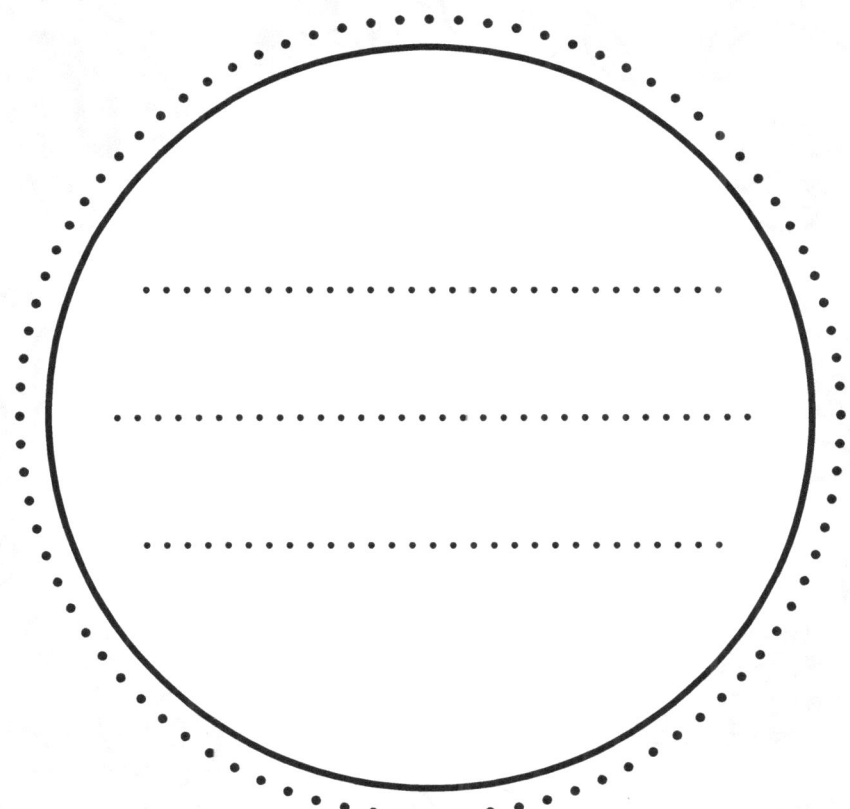

Visit my website and get a lot of free coloring books and coloring pages (section: freebies)

*USA/English Books:*

**www.monsoonpublishing.com**

*German Books:*

**www.monsoonpublishing.de**

or join my facebook groups

IMPRESSUM
Monsoon Publishing LLC:
Info@monsoonpublishing.de
www.monsoonpublishing.de
**facebook.com/monsoonpublishingllc**

IMPRESS
Monsoon Publishing LLC
nfo@monsoonpublishing.com
www.monsoonpublishing.com
**facebook.com/monsoonpublishingusa**

www.ingramcontent.com/pod-product-compliance
Lightning Source LLC
Chambersburg PA
CBHW081005140626
46546CB00019B/3441